THE SOUL OF THE WORLD

A M O D E R N

THE SOUL OF THE WORLD

Edited by
Phil Cousineau

Photographs by
Eric Lawton

HarperSanFrancisco
A Division of HarperCollins*Publishers*

*Harper San Francisco and the authors, in association with
the Rainforest Action Network, will facilitate the planting of two trees
for every one tree used in the manufacture of this book.*

Copyright credits are printed at the back of the book.

THE SOUL OF THE WORLD: *A Modern Book of Hours.* Text copyright © 1993 by Phil Cousineau. Photographs copyright © 1993 by Eric Lawton. All rights reserved. Printed in Hong Kong. No part of this book may be used or reproduced in any manner whatsoever without written permission except in the case of brief quotations embodied in critical articles and reviews. For information address HarperCollins Publishers, 10 East 53rd Street, New York, NY 10022.

FIRST EDITION   Book design by Detta Penna

Library of Congress Cataloging-in-Publication Data
The soul of the world : a modern book of hours / Phil Cousineau, editor ; with photographs
    by Eric Lawton. — 1st ed.
        p.   cm.
    ISBN 0–06–251004–5 (pbk.)
1. Meditations.   2. Photography, artistic.   I. Cousineau, Phil.   II. Lawton, Eric.
BL624.2.S68   1993
291.4'3—dc20   92—53902
                                                                              CIP

95 96 97 ❖ HCP-HK 10 9 8 7 6 5 4 3

To my mother, Rosemary M. Cousineau, for giving me faith in the soul of the world.

Phil Cousineau

To my parents, Vira and Leo Lawton, who gave me curiosity and a wandering spirit;

To my wife, Gail, who, after my years of seeking throughout the world, showed me what I was looking for; and

To our child, Rebecca, so new to this world, to whom we hope to give all that we have seen.

Eric Lawton

The new work of art does not consist of making a living or producing an objet d'art or in self-therapy, but in finding a new soul. The new era is the era of spiritual creativity . . . and soul-making.

Henry Miller, *The Wisdom of the Heart*

CONTENTS

Acknowledgments

Introduction

Sunday

Monday

Tuesday

Wednesday

Thursday

Friday

Saturday

The Hidden Image

Photographs

Credits

ACKNOWLEDGMENTS

I would like to convey my deep gratitude to all those hands and hearts who helped in the shaping of the ideas and images of this marvelous collaboration, especially:

Eric Lawton, David Darling, and John Densmore, for their soulful collaboration with me in "The Mythic Image" workshops at Esalen Institute, which inspired this book.

Father Theodore Walters, S.J., for his spiritual guidance during my dark night of the soul, and his keen insights into the tradition of the medieval Book of Hours.

Paul Cousineau, my brother-in-arms, for his long-reaching support and trickster soul.

Tom Grady, my editor, for his leap of faith in the revival of contemplative books such as this; Detta Penna, for her illuminated design; and Jo Beaton, for her soul and inspiration.

Phil Cousineau

I would like to thank those who inspired and nurtured the creation of this book. First of all is Phil Cousineau, for without his creativity, unique vision, and perseverence this book would not exist. Our collaboration over the years has been a constant source of renewal for me.

My thanks also to Arthur Secunda, my friend and mentor, whose great talent, support, and encouragement I have deeply appreciated; to Rand DeMattei, whose friendship and countless hours of editing helped me to find the right photographs for this project; to Richard Kasuyama for his skill and craftsmanship; to John Densmore and David Darling, whose improvisational genius added new dimensions to my perception of my work.

I wish to thank Tom Grady, Jamie Sue Brooks, Kevin Bentley, and all those at Harper San Francisco, for their patience, understanding, and guidance in the creation of this book.

To my wife, Gail, who spent long, late hours while pregnant to help me to realize this project and whose love and understanding have been an inspiration.

And finally, to all those whom I have encountered in years of journeys throughout the world, in whose warmth, sharing, and hospitality I have experienced a sense of the collective face that is the soul of the world.

Eric Lawton

INTRODUCTION

If the world is, as the poet said, a "vale of soul-making," then perhaps the soul is a vale of world-making. Soul: the blue fire: the fire-roots: the roots of the gods: the gods of the hidden forces: the forces behind the world: the world of soul.

And so the mystery turns. Something strange comes our way, a shadow from the depths, a hint of another dimension, the pulse of the unfathomable. Once nudged, we know we will not sleep until we have found a name for it, a place where we can hear an echo of it, an image for that infernal part of us that is immortal.

Some call it the sacred; some, the holy. There, where we wonder with wild hearts, the temple is built, the temple in which we *con-template* (literally, "make a temple with") the depths. For some, the soul's plunge into the silent hours is deep inside the temple of the earth; for others, an oak grove grown from a scattering of acorns or a stone poem of cathedral where the spirit can rise like incense. And there, where the inner and outer forces meet, is the soul of the world.

No one really knows what the soul is, but tremble forth it does and, just as mysteriously, shudders away again. To paraphrase Gandhi, nothing that we say about it matters, but it's very important that we say it. The question of the soul is precisely this: a questing, a critical movement to *re*search, *re*imagine, *re*discover what it means to live in the depths; to respond to the godless hours, the soulless days, the spiritless years; to recover the sacred.

So we have business with this shadowy presence called soul. Shadow, breath, psyche, heat, vortex, whirlpool, the celestial light, the primal sphere, the essential nature, the life force, the beveled edge between spirit and world, the frontier of meaning, a bird taking flight, a serpent slipping out of the nether world, Plato's rider on the galloping horse, Saint Teresa of Avila's "interior castle," or simply, as Christ said, wherever our treasure is: *soul*.

"Riddle me this," asks the sphinx. "What was never born but dies again and again and can be found in child, stone, or stars?" History abounds with the confounding search for the paradoxical image of *that which does not change* in a constantly changing world. One Greek tradition holds that the soul is to be found in the head; another has it attached to the body at various joints, an idea also found in Siberia, South America, and West Africa. Ancient Egyptians thought the soul to be in the tongue, the rudder of the body. Eastern traditions commonly place it in the belly. Souls may also exist in the spinal marrow, the seminal fluid, brain, blood, hair, and nails.

The soul is the name for the unifying principle, power, or energy that is at the center of our being. To be in touch with soul means going back to the sacred source, the site of life-releasing energy, the activating force of life, the god-grounds; to venture forth and confront the world in all its marvelous and terrifying forces, to make sacred our hours here; to learn to pay such supreme attention to the world that eternity blazes into time with our holy longing. Soul-making, this.

What stirs in us stirs in the world. Venturing forth to bring the two together is, in the felicitous phrasing of Joseph Campbell, "the soul's high adventure." It is the movement from the remote pond of self-reflection that Narcissus found so enchanting to the reenchantment of the world, a revisioning of the fallen image of a dying earth to an earth rising, an image of the living planet that the ancients called Gaia.

Through such bold revisioning, soul as wayfarer, sojourner, lives up to its tantalizing destiny, which is to explore and contemplate the stories, smells, and stones, the *soulscapes* of the world. Seeing in a sacred manner— out of the corner of our third eye, so to speak—allows us to see what is in the numinous shadows of those archaic gateways—waterfalls, groves, mesas, canyons, springs, grottoes, caves, glaciers—sites revealed as sacred through generations of pilgrimages, vision quests, rituals, and monumental building: *Chaco Canyon, Lascaux, Delphi, Machu Picchu, Glastonbury, Palenque, Chartres.*

From the "white-maned rivers" of Yosemite Valley to the miraculous flying buttresses of the Chartres cathedral, monuments both heaven-inspired and human-engineered celebrate the whirling dervish energies of the earth, sanctify the powers that can vitalize our spiritual life if we choose to notice them as sacred. For millennia these sites have been regarded as holy grounds, not out of dogma or folkish superstition, but because of the actual experiences people have had there: the cures, the healings, the visions, the rites of fertility and burial, the encounters with the gods. These are our soul-sites: the silencing sanctuaries that heal and replenish us, urge us to remember not to be spirited away from this world but to plunge back into its beauty. *Guilin, Giza, Connemara, Kauai, Algonquin, Angkor Wat, the Himalaya.*

"All living things are *interwoven* each with the other," said Marcus Aurelius; "the tie is sacred, and nothing, or next to nothing, is alien to anything else." Revisioning, then respectfully reentering, the world is the relearning of the *genius loci,* the spirit of place, that the ancient Greeks spoke of. It is sensing the divine in nature, as the biologist René Dubos reminds us, with that which is divine within us, by the god within. Places where we strike a chord with the music of the spheres, where we display an attitude of gratitude, a reverie of reverence. Places where we feel compelled to ask the land what its evolving story is, where we align ourselves with its primordial energies; places where we can "walk our talk," where we place the soles of our feet on the soul of the world: the *Black Hills, the Brazilian rain forest, the Red Sea, Crete, Mount Fuji, Darjeeling.*

In this way will we, with Thoreau, find a way to "Read not the times, read the Eternities," and rest in the grace of the world. There where we sense all of creation trembling, as did Isak Dinesen in Africa, where we hear the stillness in the heartbeat of the world, as Henry Miller heard it at Epidaurus, where the universe becomes our companion, as Basho recommended on his narrow road to the far provinces of Japan. Then when we no longer feel ourselves inconsolably alone, nothing but a stranger in this world. Only then shall we be with all the world—there where we stretch our soul.

Long have we tried to read eternity into the world, but rarely has the story of the pilgrimage of the soul been rendered as remarkably as it was in medieval Europe. During the traumatic upheaval of the late Middle Ages, the rise of the middle class, increasing literacy, and widening prosperity made possible a revolution in bookmaking. Beyond the musty scriptoria of the clergy, more books were produced than at any time since classical antiquity. And none was more prized than the gloriously illuminated manuscript called the Book of Hours. For the next 250 years, these lavish Latin prayer books were the most popular books of the day, medieval best-sellers intended not for the clergy but for ordinary men and women.

The Book of Hours derived its name from the Hours of the Virgin, a passel of devotional prayers and paintings to Mary that were offered according to the canonical hours. In this time before time had been mechanized, medieval life revolved around the Church's canonical hours of the day: *Matins* (midnight), *Lauds* (sunrise), *Prime* (6:00 A.M.), *Terce* (9:00 A.M.), *Sext* (noon), *None* (3:00 P.M.), *Vespers* (sunset), and *Compline* (9:00 P.M.). By ritualizing private meditation, the Book of Hours helped laypeople focus on what was sacred about the hours of their everyday life. Gazing upon iconic images became a form of devotion; reading inspired words was like listening to Gregorian chant. With image and word put together in the miracle of a simplified prayer book you could have a perpetual conversation with the Virgin or the saints.

What the cathedrals are to architecture and the "Ave Maria" is to music, the Book of Hours is to literature and painting. Often described as "cathedrals in the palm of the hand," the Book of Hours offers a myriad of stained-glass window views into the medieval world, both cultural and religious. Through this proscenium, the divine mystery of the soul's relationship with God could be visualized, and by the holy act of naming the hours and the ritual contemplation of their own often personally selected prayers and pictures, secular time was sanctified for ordinary people as it had long been for the privileged few in the cloistered monasteries. The democratization of religion had begun.

Contemplation of beauty is the consolation of the world. The soul needs the slow absorbing of beauty just as plants long for the sun and the sea craves the moon. Deep contemplation of beauty in the scudding clouds over an ancient Mayan temple, the shimmering blue-white light of Vermeer's portrait *A Woman in Blue Reading a Letter,* the deep black god-tracks of Old English in the hoary pages of *Beowulf* is still our most creative human response to the shuddering of the soul.

All my life I've been intrigued by the marvelous. From the lightning-bolted green skies of Michigan electrical storms and the eldritch echoes of the Latin High Mass of my boyhood, to the blue-veined glaciers in the Swiss Alps and legend-barnacled walls of Troy of my wanderlust years as a young man, I've been tracking down the marvels of the world. And always after every encounter with the wonders of the world came a further wonder: How can I keep alive the astounding moments of my life so that I might withstand the turbulence, the soul-breaking moments?

Out of that question came a desire finally to distill into a single volume the notebooks and journals I've filled and the great books I've encountered: a spiritual distillation of wisdom words accented by images I would eagerly return to over and over, a soul-pack, a pocket cathedral—what travelers in medieval Europe called a *vade mecum,* a "go-with-me" that they carried for contemplation—a book that might even connect my soul and the soul of the world.

Much in this spirit, Emerson once wrote, "Make your own Bible. Select and collect all the words and sentences that in all your reading have been to you like the blast of triumph out of Shakespeare, Seneca, Moses, John and Paul." In other words, collect chapters for your own Book of Soul; consider phrases that have shivered in your bones; practice an art of life crafted with sacred attention on the persistent images of what Thomas Berry calls "the grand liturgy of the universe." Think globally, act locally, contemplate hourly.

The Soul of the World as a contemplative modern Book of Hours emerges from my own urge to juxtapose the words that have been branded into me with indelible images that might create the *third thing:* the unpredictable energy of art. Through my work with the photographer Eric Lawton I have found a brother in this search for the seizing and bringing home of the decisive moment, the hidden image, the secret beauty in the forgotten shadows of the world. His photographs have been captured with a keen eye, a still heart, and an active soul. His images, like the megalithic stones he has journeyed to from Stonehenge to Machu Picchu, are amplifiers of the numinous energies of the earth, images hinting at the sacred configuration of the universe. Eric's mandalic images call to us again and again to review them, not simply out of admiration, nor to lead us out of this world with lofty thoughts, but to lead us back into it with grounding feelings.

The Soul of the World comes out of the long tradition of praise-singing. It is a nod to the Australian belief that "an unsung land will die"; a gesture to the notion that beauty gives us courage; an echo of Scriabin's revelation that "the universe resounds with the joyful cry I am!"; a kind of makeshift lens through which we can refocus on the gorgeous chaos, the terrible beauty, the genuine soul of the world.

Through beguiling connections come exultant juxtapositions, such as Black Elk's vision of the Black Hills of North Dakota with a sunrise over the Himalaya, Anna Akmatova's revelation about "the secret of secrets" with a remote fishing shack in Virginia, the long sigh of an old Navajo chant with the whirling winds rising over the inscrutable stones of Salisbury Plain.

Our common destiny is a dream within the dream of a common story, an enigma waiting for a creative response to the pressing mystery hovering above us, a humble understanding of what the physicist Sir Arthur Eddington meant when he said at the end of his life, "Something unknown is doing we don't know what."

For the world is many souls deep. Try looking into the dark wedge of God's shadow cast on the peaks and vales when the sun is setting as the moon rises: within the shadows of the world might appear your own soul, the soul of your fiercest desire, the desire for stretching your deepest contemplation, your contemplation of the old riddle of immortality, the immortality of the blue fire, the fire of hidden beauty, the beauty of your most sacred attention, the attention to making holy the hours, the hours of reading the soul of the world.

Phil Cousineau
San Francisco

SUNDAY

Yea, the first morning of Creation wrote what the
Last Dawn of Reckoning shall read.

Omar Khayyám

Matins

When I speak of darkness, I am referring to a lack
of knowing. It is a lack of knowing that includes
everything you do not know or else that you have
forgotten, whatever is altogether dark for you
because you do not see it with your spiritual eye.
And for this reason it is not called a cloud of the
air, but rather a cloud of unknowing that is
between you and your God.

The Cloud of Unknowing,
(anonymous English monk, fourteenth century)

Chandrakot, Nepal

Lauds

The heavens declare God's glory
and the magnificence of what made them.
Each new dawn is a miracle;
each new sky fills with beauty.

Their testimony speaks to the whole world
and reaches to the ends of the earth.

In them is a path for the sun,
who steps forth handsome as a bridegroom
and rejoices like an athlete as he runs.

He starts at one end of the heavens
and circles to the other end,
and nothing can hide from his heat.

Psalm 19:1–6

Pokhara, Nepal

SUNDAY

Prime

In the beginning was the Tao.
All things issue from it;
all things return to it.

To find the origin,
trace back the manifestations,
When you recognize the children
and find the mother,
you will be free of sorrow.

If you close your mind in judgments
and traffic with desires,
your heart will be troubled.
If you keep your mind from judging
and aren't led by the senses,
your heart will find peace.

Seeing into darkness is clarity.
Knowing how to yield is strength.
Use your own light
and return to the source of light.
This is called practicing eternity.

Lao-tzu, Chinese (c. 600 B.C.)

Taos, New Mexico

Terce

Every day is a god, each day is a god, and holiness
holds forth in time. I worship each god, I praise
each day splintered down, and wrapped in time
like a husk, a husk of many colors spreading, at
dawn fast over the mountains split.

Annie Dillard, American (1945–   )

Machapuchare, Nepal

Sext

There is nothing but water in the holy pools. I know, I have been
   swimming in them.
All the gods sculpted of wood or ivory can't say a word.
I know, I have been crying out to them.
The Sacred Books of the East are nothing but words.
I looked through their covers one day sideways.
What Kabir talks of is only what he has lived through.
If you have not lived through something, it is not true.

Kabīr, Indian (1440–1518)

Taj Mahal, Agra, India

SUNDAY

None

The earth is to the sun,
as the soul is to God.
The earth,
at any point,
can be located by its relationship
        to the sun.

The earth has a scaffold of stones
and trees. In the same way is a person formed:
        flesh is the earth,
        the bones are the trees and stones.

The soul is the firmament of the organism, then.
In the manner in which the soul permeates the body with its
energy, it causes and consummates all human action.

The person that does good works is indeed
this orchard bearing good fruit. And this
is just like the earth with its ornamentation
of stone and blossoming trees.

> Hildegard of Bingen,
> German (1098–1179)

Suzhou, China

Vespers

In the point of rest at the center of our being, we encounter a world where all things are at rest in the same way. Then a tree becomes a mystery, a cloud a revelation, each man a cosmos of whose riches we can only catch glimpses. The life of simplicity is simple, but it opens to us a book in which we never get beyond the first syllable.

Dag Hammarskjöld,
Swedish (1905–1961)

Huangshan, China

SUNDAY

Compline

There is not as much wilderness
out there as I wish there were.
There is more inside
than you think.

David Brower,
American (1912–   )

The universe has been quite literally writing upon
humans for many thousands of years, and our
alphabets are among the trails that nature has
carved in order to cross our minds. Wild lands have
cut deeper trails in my life than I will ever be able
to make in the forest.

Joe Meeker,
American (1932–   )

Huangshan, China

MONDAY

Call the world if you please, "The Vale of Soul
Making." Then you will find out the use of the
world.

John Keats

Matins

When I would recreate myself, I seek the darkest
wood, the thickest and most interminable, and to
the citizen, most dismal swamp. I enter the swamp
as a sacred place—a *sanctum sanctorum*. There is
the strength, the marrow of Nature.

> Henry David Thoreau,
> American (1817–1862)

Yangshuo, China

MONDAY

Lauds

Then I was standing on the highest mountain of them all, and round about beneath me was the whole hoop of the world. And while I stood there I saw more than I can tell and I understood more than I saw; for I was seeing in a sacred manner the shapes of all things in the spirit, and the shape of all shapes as they must live together like one being. And I saw the sacred hoop of my people was one of the many hoops that made one circle, wide as daylight and as starlight, and in the center grew one mighty flowering tree to shelter all the children of one mother and one father. And I saw that it was holy. . . .

But anywhere is the center of the world.

Black Elk,
Oglala Sioux (1863–1950)

Kanchenjunga, from Darjeeling, India

MONDAY

Prime

We have seen the highest circle of spiraling powers. We have named this circle God. We might have
given it any other name we wished: Abyss, Mystery,
Absolute Darkness, Absolute Light, Matter, Spirit,
Ultimate Hope, Ultimate Despair, Silence. But we
have named it God because only this name, for primordial reasons, can stir our hearts profoundly.
And this deeply felt emotion is indispensable if we
are to touch, body with body, the dread essence
beyond logic.

Nikos Kazantzakis,
Greek (1885–1957)

Sinai Desert

MONDAY

Terce

"God is the shadow of man," was commented upon
by the Baal Shem as follows: just as a shadow follows the gestures and motions of the body, God
follows those of the soul. If man is charitable, God
will be charitable too. The name of man's secret is
God, and the name of God's secret is none other
than the one invented by man: love. Who loves,
loves God. . . . And what is love if not a creative
act, in which two beings fuse into a single con-
sciousness scarred and healed a thousand times?
Love's mystery resides in oneness, and so does
God's. "Whatever is above is also down below."
Between the present concrete world and the other,
the one to come, there is a link as between source
and reflection. God does not oppose humanity, and
man, though vulnerable and ephemeral, can attain
immortality in the passing moment. In man's universe, everything is connected because nothing is
without meaning.

Elie Wiesel,
American (1928–   )

Yangshuo, China

MONDAY

Sext

Nature-love as Emerson knew it, and as
Wordsworth knew it, and as any of the choicer
spirits of our time have known it, has distinctly a
religious value. It does not come to a man or a
woman who is wholly absorbed in selfish or world-
ly or material ends. Except ye become in a measure
as little children, ye cannot enter the kingdom of
Nature—as Audubon entered it, as Thoreau entered
it, as Bryant and Amiel entered it, and as all those
enter it who make it a resource in their lives and an
instrument of their culture. The forms and creeds of
religion change, but the sentiment of religion—the
wonder and reverence and love we feel in the presence of the inscrutable universe—persist. . . . If we
do not go to church as much as did our fathers, we
go to the woods much more, and are much more
inclined to make a temple of them than they were.

John Burroughs,
American (1837–1921)

Kalalau Valley, Kauai, Hawaii

MONDAY

None

Clambering up the Cold Mountain path,
The Cold Mountain trail goes on and on:
The long gorge choked with scree and boulders,
The wide creek, the mist-blurred grass.
The moss is slippery, though there's been no rain
The pine sings, but there's no wind.
Who can leap the world's ties
And sit with me among the white clouds?

Han-shan,
Chinese (fl. 627–649)

Huangshan, China

MONDAY

Vespers

Up in this high air, you breathed easily, drawing in
a vital assurance and lightness of heart. In the high-
lands, you woke up in the morning and thought:
"Here I am, where I ought to be."

Isak Dinesen,
Danish (1885–1962)

Masai Mara, Kenya

MONDAY

Compline

And who has seen the moon, who has not seen
Her rise from out the chamber of the deep,
Flushed and grand and naked, as from the chamber
Of finished bridegroom, seen her rise and throw
Confession of delight upon the wave,
Littering the waves with her own superscription
Of bliss, till all her lambent beauty shakes toward us
Spread out and known at last, and we are sure
That beauty is a thing beyond the grave,
That perfect, bright experience never falls
To nothingness, and time will dim the moon
Sooner than our full consummation here
In this odd life will tarnish or pass away.

D. H. Lawrence,
English (1885–1930)

Taos Pueblo, New Mexico

MONDAY

TUESDAY

The contemplation of Eternity maketh the Soul
immortal.

Thomas Traherne

Matins

The wooing of the Earth thus implies much more than converting the wilderness into humanized environments. It means also preserving natural environments in which to experience mysteries transcending daily life and from which to recapture, in a Proustian kind of remembrance, the awareness of the cosmic forces that have shaped humankind.

René Dubos,
American (1901–1982)

Chandrakot, Nepal

TUESDAY

Lauds

Some nights, stay up till dawn.
As the moon sometimes does for the sun.
Be a full bucket pulled up the dark way
of a well, then lifted out into light.

Something opens our wings. Something
makes boredom and hurt disappear.
Someone fills the cup in front of us.
We taste only sacredness.

Jalāl ad-Dīn ar-Rūmī,
Persian (c. 1207–1273)

Guilin, China

TUESDAY

Prime

Return me, oh sun,
to my wild destiny,
rain of the ancient wood,
bring me back to the aroma and the swords
that fall from the sky,
the solitary peace of pasture and rock,
the damp at the river-margins,
the smell of the larch tree,
the wind alive like a heart
beating in the crowded restlessness
of the towering araucaria.

Earth, give me back your pure gifts,
the towers of silence which rose
from the solemnity of their roots.
I want to go back to being what I have not been,
and learn to go back from such deeps
that amongst all natural things
I could live or not live; it does not matter
to be one stone more, the dark stone,
the pure stone which the river bears away.

Pablo Neruda,
Chilean (1904–1973)

Cayucos, California

TUESDAY

Terce

I live my life in growing orbits
Which move out over the things of the world.
Perhaps I can never achieve the last,
but that will be my attempt.

I am circling around God, the ancient tower,
and I have been circling for a thousand years,
and I still don't know if I am a falcon, or a storm,
or a great song.

Rainer Maria Rilke,
German (1875–1926)

Wuxi, China

TUESDAY

Sext

Wayfarer, the only way
is your footsteps, there is no other.
Wayfarer, there is no way,
you make the way as you go.
As you go, you make the way
and stopping to look behind,
you see the path that your feet
will travel again.
Wayfarer, there is no way—
only foam trails in the sea.

Antonio Machado,
Spanish (1875–1939)

Inca Trail, Peru

None

If my soul could get away from this so-called
prison, be granted all the list of attributes generally
bestowed on spirits, my first ramble on spirit-wings
would not be among the volcanoes of the moon.
Nor should I follow the sunbeams to their sources
in the sun. I should hover about the beauty of our
own good star. I should not go moping among the
tombs, nor around the artificial desolation of men. I
should study Nature's laws in all their crossings and
unions; I should follow magnetic streams to their
source and follow the shores of our magnetic
oceans. I should go among the rays of the aurora,
and follow them to their beginnings, and study
their dealings and communions with other powers
and expressions of matter. And I should go to the
very center of our globe and read the whole splen-
did page from the beginning.

John Muir,
American (1838–1914)

Death Valley, California

Vespers

I enjoy the silence in a church before the service
more than any sermon.

> Ralph Waldo Emerson,
> American (1803–1882)

There is nothing so much like God in all the
universe as silence.

> Meister Eckhart,
> German (c. 1260–1327?)

Copenhagen, Denmark

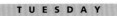

TUESDAY

Compline

A Night—there lay the Days between—
The Day that was Before—
And Day that was Behind—were one—
And now—'twas Night—was here—

Slow—Night—that must be watched away—
As Grains upon a shore—
Too imperceptible to note—
Till it be night—no more—

Emily Dickinson,
American (1830–1886)

Stonehenge, England

TUESDAY

WEDNESDAY

You can only go halfway
into the darkest forest; then you are coming out
the other side.

Chinese proverb

Matins

Midway along our road of life I woke
to find myself in a secret dark wood,
for I had lost the narrow path. To evoke

what it was like—how hard, I barely could.
This wood was savage, dense and strange! The thought
of it renews those fears that I withstood,

a place so bitter, only to be caught
in death is worse. Yet there I found my share
of good, so now I'll tell what else it brought.

I cannot rightly say how I came there,
I was so drugged with sleep the moment when
I lost the true way, wandering unaware,

Yet when . . . I looked up, saw the hill's wings with their clean
early light cast from the planet whose sight
leads men straightly on every road. The scene

diminished and I felt the force of fright
lessen in the lake of my heart, that fear
I felt so piteously throughout the night.

Dante Alighieri,
Italian (1265–1321)

Pfeiffer Beach, Big Sur, California

Lauds

At each moment she starts upon a long journey and at each moment reaches her end. . . . All is eternally present in her, for she knows neither past nor future.
For her the present is eternity.

Yet not in torpor would I find,
Awe is the finest portion of mankind.
However scarce the world may make this sense—
In awe one feels profoundly the immense.

Johann Wolfgang von Goethe,
German (1749–1832)

Salisbury Plain, England

Prime

Toward dawn he dreamed that he had concealed himself in one of the naves of the Clementine Library. A librarian wearing dark glasses asked him: "What are you looking for?" Hladik answered: "I am looking for God." The librarian said to him: "God is in one of the pages of the four hundred thousand volumes of the Clementine. My fathers and the fathers of my fathers have searched for this letter. I have grown blind seeking it." He removed his glasses, and Hladik saw his eyes, which were dead. A reader came in to return an atlas. "This atlas is worthless," he said, and handed it to Hladik, who opened it at random. He saw a map of India as in a daze. A ubiquitous voice said to him: "The time of your labor has been granted." At this Hladik awoke.

Jorge Luis Borges,
Argentinian (1899–1986)

Jutland Lighthouse, Denmark

WEDNESDAY

Terce

A land not mine, still
forever memorable,
the waters of its ocean
chill and fresh.

Sand on the bottom whiter than chalk,
and the air drunk, like wine,
late sun lays bare
the rosy limbs of the pine trees.

Sunset in the ethereal waves:
I cannot tell if the day
is ending, or the world, or if
the secret of secrets is inside me again.

Anna Akmatova,
Russian (1889–1966)

Chincoteague, Virginia

WEDNESDAY

Sext

And he showed me a pure river of water of life,
clear as crystal, proceeding out of the throne of
God and of the Lamb. In the midst of the street of
it, and on either side of the river, was there the tree
of life, which bare twelve manner of fruits, and
yielded her fruit every month: and the leaves of the
tree were for the healing of the nations.

The Revelation of Saint John
(22:1–2, KJV)

Hanalei, Kauai, Hawaii

None

Then he was told:
Remember what you have seen,
because everything forgotten
returns to the circling winds.

Lines from a Navajo chant

Stonehenge, England

WEDNESDAY

Vespers

The only true wisdom lives far from mankind, out
in the great loneliness, and it can be reached only
through suffering. Privation and suffering alone
can open the mind of a man to all that is hidden
to others.

Igjugarjuk,
Caribou Eskimo shaman
(early twentieth century)

The great sea stirs me.
The great sea sets me adrift,
it sways me like the weed
on a river-stone.

The sky's height stirs me.
The strong wind blows through my mind.
It carries me with it,
so I shake with joy.

Uvavnuk,
Iglulik Eskimo shaman
(early twentieth century)

Pastoruri Glacier, Huascarán, Peru

WEDNESDAY

Compline

Away I turn to the holy, the unspeakable, the secretive Night. Over there, far, lies the world—sunken in a deep pit—desert, its place lonely. In the heart's strings, deep sadness blows. In dewdrops I'll sink and mix with the ashes.

Novalis,
German (1772–1801)

Dhampus, Nepal

THURSDAY

My dancing, my drinking, and singing
weave me the mat on which my soul will sleep
in the world of spirits.

Old Man of Halmahera, Indonesia

Matins

When you are old and grey and full of sleep,
And nodding by the fire, take down this book,
And slowly read, and dream of the soft look
Your eyes had once, and of their shadows deep;

How many loved your moments of glad grace,
And loved your beauty with love false or true,
But one man loved the pilgrim soul in you,
And loved the sorrows of your changing face;

And bending down beside the glowing bars,
Murmur, a little sadly, how Love fled
And paced upon the mountains overhead
And hid his face amid a crowd of stars.

William Butler Yeats,
Irish (1856–1939)

Santa Fe, New Mexico

THURSDAY

Lauds

The shore is an ancient world, for as long as there has been an earth and sea there has been this place of the meeting of land and water. Yet it is a world that keeps alive the sense of continuing creation and of the relentless drive of life. Each time that I enter it, I gain some new awareness of its beauty and its deeper meanings, sensing that intricate fabric of life by which one creature is linked with another, and each with its surroundings. . . .

There is a common thread that links these scenes and memories—the spectacle of life in all its varied manifestations as it has appeared, evolved, and sometimes died out. Underlying the beauty of the spectacle there is meaning and significance. It is the elusiveness of that meaning that haunts us, that sends us again and again into the natural world where the key to the riddle is hidden. It sends us back to the edge of the sea, where the drama of life played its first scene on earth and perhaps even its prelude; where the forces of evolution are at work today, as they have been since the appearance of what we know as life; and where the spectacle of living creatures faced by the cosmic realities of their world is crystal clear.

Rachel Carson,
American (1907–1964)

Caribbean, Bahamas

Prime

Gratitude to Mother Earth, sailing through night and day—
    and to her soil: rich, rare, and sweet
        in our minds so be it

Gratitude to Plants, the sun-facing light-changing leaf
    and fine root-hairs; standing still through wind
    and rain; their dance is in the flowing spiral grain
        in our minds so be it. . . .

Gratitude to Wild Beings, our brothers, teaching secrets,
    freedoms, and ways, who share with us their milk,
    self-complete, brave, and aware
        in our minds so be it

Gratitude to Water: clouds, lakes, rivers, glaciers;
    holding or releasing; streaming through
    all our bodies salty seas
        in our minds so be it

Gratitude to the Sun: blinding pulsing light through
    trunks of trees, through mists, warming caves where
    bears and snakes sleep—he who wakes us—
        in our minds so be it

Gratitude to the Great Sky
    who holds billions of stars and goes yet beyond that—
    beyond all powers and thoughts, and yet is within us—
    Grandfather Space. The Mind is his wife.
        So be it.

Gary Snyder (after a Mohawk prayer),
American (1930–   )

Yangshuo, China

THURSDAY

Terce

Through how many dimensions and how many media will life have to pass? Down how many roads among the stars must man propel himself in search of the final secret? The journey is difficult, immense, at times impossible, yet that will not deter some of us from attempting it. We cannot know all that has happened in the past, or the reason for all of these events, any more than we can with surety discern what lies ahead. We have joined the caravan, you might say, at a certain point; we will travel as far as we can, but we cannot in one lifetime see all that we would like to see or learn all that we hunger to know. . . . I have tried to put down such miracles as can be evoked from common earth. But men see differently. I can at best report only from my own wilderness. The important thing is that each man possess such a wilderness and that he consider what marvels are to be observed there.

Loren Eisley,
American (1907–1977)

Zabriskie Point, Death Valley, California

THURSDAY

Sext

Here I am, seated, with all my words,
like a basket of green fruit, intact.
The fragments
of a thousand destroyed ancient gods
seek and draw near each other in my blood. They long
to rebuild their statue.
From their shattered mouths
a song strives to rise to my mouth,
a scent of burned resins, some gesture
of mysterious wrought stone. . . .
I look not at the submerged temples,
but only at the trees that above the ruins
move their vast shadow, with acid teeth bite
the wind as it passes. . . .
But I know: behind
my body another body crouches,
and round about me many breaths
furtively cross
like nocturnal beasts in the jungle. . . .
But I know only a few words
in the lapidary language
under which they buried my ancestor alive.

Rosario Castellanos,
Mexican (1925–1974)

Machu Picchu, Peru

None

Sometimes a man humbles himself in his heart, sub-
mits the visible to the power to see, and seeks to
return to his source. He seeks, he finds, and he
returns home. . . . To return to the source of things,
one has to travel in the opposite direction. . . .
And you, what do you seek?

René Daumal,
French (1908–1944)

Punakha Monastery, Bhutan

Vespers

Dew evaporates
    and all our world
is dew . . . so dear,
so refreshing, so fleeting

Issa, on the death of his child,
Japanese (1763–1827)

In this world
the living grow fewer
the dead increase—
how much longer must I
carry this body of grief?

Ono No Komachi,
Japanese (b. 834?)

Hiroshima, Japan

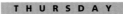

THURSDAY

Compline

I am the boundless ocean.

This way and that,
The wind, blowing where it will,
Drives the ship of the world.

But I am not shaken.

I am the unbounded deep
In whom the waves of all the worlds
Naturally rise and fall.

But I do not rise or fall.

I am the infinite deep
In whom all the worlds
Appear to rise.

Beyond all form,
Forever still.

Even so am I.

Ashtavakra Gita,
unknown Hindu master
(fifth or fourth century B.C.)

Hanalei, Kauai, Hawaii

THURSDAY

FRIDAY

If the soul could have known God without the world,
the world would never have been created.

Meister Eckhart

Matins

A white explorer in Africa, anxious to press ahead
with his journey, paid his porters for a series of
forced marches. But they, almost within reach of
their destination, set down their bundles and
refused to budge. No amount of extra payment
would convince them otherwise. They said they
had to wait for their souls to catch up.

Bruce Chatwin,
English (1940–1989)

Suzhou, China

FRIDAY

Lauds

God loves a curved universe.

> Buckminster Fuller,
> American (1895–1983)

God is an intelligible sphere whose center is every-
where and circumference nowhere.

> *The Book of the Twenty-four Philosophers,*
> (twelfth-century Latin hermetic text)

Death Valley, California

FRIDAY

Prime

Fold your wings, my soul,
those wings you had spread wide
to soar to the terrestrial peaks
where the light is most ardent:
it is for you simply to wait
the descent of the Fire—supposing it to be willing
to take possession of you.

Pierre Teilhard de Chardin,
French (1881–1955)

Sounion, Greece

FRIDAY

Terce

I've known rivers:
I've known rivers ancient as the world and older than the
    flow of human blood in human veins.

My soul has grown deep like the rivers.

I bathed in the Euphrates when dawns were young.
I built my hut near the Congo and it lulled me to sleep.
I looked upon the Nile and raised the pyramids above it.
I heard the singing of the Mississippi when Abe Lincoln went down
    to New Orleans, and I've seen its muddy bosom turn all
    golden in the sunset.

I've known rivers:
Ancient, dusky rivers.

My soul has grown deep like rivers.

Langston Hughes,
African American (1902–1967)

Lake Titicaca, Peru

FRIDAY

Sext

For I have learned
To look on nature, not as in the hour
Of thoughtless youth; but hearing oftentimes
The still, sad music of humanity,
Nor harsh nor grating, though of ample power
To chasten and subdue. And I have felt
A presence that disturbs me with the joy
Of elevated thoughts; a sense of sublime
Of something far more deeply interfused,
Whose dwelling is the light of setting suns,
And the round ocean and the living air,
And the blue sky, and in the mind of man:
A motion and a spirit, that impels
All thinking things, all objects of all thought,
And rolls through all things. Therefore am I still
A lover of the meadows and the woods
And mountains, and of all that we behold
From this green earth, of all the mighty world
Of eye, and ear—both what they half create,
And what they perceive, well pleased to recognise
In nature and the language of the sense
The anchor of my purest thoughts, the nurse,
The guide, the guardian of my heart and soul
Of all my moral being.

William Wordsworth, English (1770–1850)

The Louvre, Paris, France

FRIDAY

None

The river of our perceptions continues to flow,
but now, in the sunlight of our awareness, it flows
peacefully, and we are serene. The relation
between the river of perceptions and the sun
of awareness is not the same as that of an actual
river and the actual sun. . . . But when the sun of
awareness shines on the river of our perceptions,
the mind is transformed. Both river and sun are of
the same nature.

Thich Nhat Hanh,
Vietnamese (1926–   )

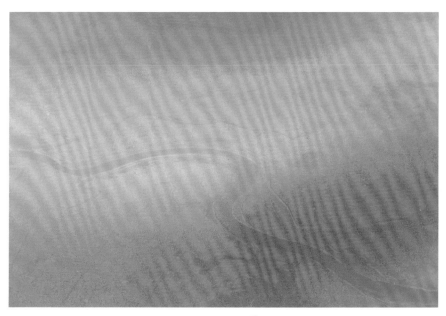

Yangtze River, China

Vespers

Standing by my bed

In gold sandals
Dawn that very
moment awoke me

Hesperus, you herd
home whatever
Dawn's light dispersed

You herd sheep—herd
goats—herd children
home to their mothers

Sappho of Lesbos,
Greek (c. 612–c. 565 B.C.)

Paro Valley, Bhutan

Compline

Penetrating so many secrets,
we cease to believe in the unknowable.
But there it sits nevertheless,
calmly licking its chops.

H. L. Mencken,
American (1880–1956)

Guanajuato Tunnel, Mexico

SATURDAY

My soul's the present shadow of a presence gone.

Fernando Pessoa

Matins

When the full fields begin to smell of sunrise
And the valleys sing in their sleep,
The pilgrim moon pours over the solemn darkness
Her waterfalls of silence,
And then departs, up the long avenue of trees.

The stars hide, in the glade, their lights, like tears,
Baying in eastward mysteries of distance,
Where fire flares, somewhere, over a sink of cities.

New kindle in the windows of this ladyhouse, my soul,
Your childish, clear awakeness:
Burn in the country night
Your wise and sleepless lamp.
For, from the frowning tower, the windy belfry,
Sudden the bells come, bridegrooms,
And fill the echoing dark with love and fear. . . .

Wake in the cloisters of the lonely night, my soul, my sister,
Where the apostles gather, who were, one time, scattered,
And mourn God's blood in the place of His betrayal,
And weep with Peter at the triple cock-crow.

Thomas Merton,
American (1915–1968)

Dordogne Valley, France

Lauds

This is thy hour O Soul, thy free flight into the wordless.
Away from books, away from art, the day erased, the lesson done.
Thee fully forth emerging silent, gazing, pondering the themes
   thou lovest best,
Night, sleep, death and the stars.

Walt Whitman,
American (1819–1892)

Santa Monica, California

SATURDAY

Prime

What is going on inside me I cannot tell. In the
sky a thousand stars are magnetized, and I am
glued by the swing of the planet to the sand.
A different weight of my body drawing me towards
many things. My dreams are more real than these
dunes, than that moon, than these presences.
My civilization is an empire more imperious than
this empire. The marvel of a house is not that it
shelters or warms a man, nor that its walls belong
to him. It is that it leaves its trace on language. Let
it remain a sign. Let it form, deep in the heart, that
obscure range from which, as waters from a spring,
are born our dreams.

Antoine de Saint-Exupéry,
French (1900–1944)

Death Valley, California

Terce

Is the soul solid, like iron?
Or is it tender and breakable, like
the wings of a moth in the beak of an owl?
Who has it, and who doesn't?
I keep looking around me.
The face of a moose is as sad as the face of Jesus.
The swan opens her white wings slowly.
In the fall, the black bear carries leaves into the darkness.
One question leads to another.
Does it have a shape? Like an iceberg?
Like the eye of a hummingbird?
Does it have one lung, like the snake and the scallop?
Why should I have it, and not the anteater
who loves her children?
Why should I have it, and not the camel?
Come to think of it, what about the maple trees?
What about the blue iris?
What about all the little stones, sitting alone in the moonlight?
What about roses, and lemons, and their shining leaves?
What about the grass?

Mary Oliver,
American (1935–   )

Graves, Virginia

SATURDAY

Sext

I call the high and light aspects of my being
spirit and the dark and heavy aspects *soul.*

Soul is at home in the deep, shaded valleys.
Heavy torpid flowers saturated with black grow
there. The rivers flow like warm syrup. They
empty into huge oceans of soul.

Spirit is a land of high, white peaks and
glittering jewel-like lakes and flowers.
Life is sparse and sounds travel great distances.

There is soul music, soul food, and soul love. . . .

People need to climb the mountain not simply
because it is there but because the soulful
divinity needs to be mated with the spirit.

Tenzin Gyatso,
fourteenth Dalai Lama of Tibet
(1936–   )

Rhumtek Monastery, Gangtok, Sikkim

SATURDAY

None

The mother of us all,
the oldest of all,
hard,
      splendid as rock

Whatever there is that is of the land
               is she
                      who nourishes it,
                      it is the Earth
                              that I sing

Whoever you are,
howsoever you come
               across her sacred ground
      you of the sea,
      you that fly,
it is she
      who nourishes you
    she,
      out of her treasures
                  Beautiful children
                  beautiful harvests
                    are achieved from you
                    The giving of life itself,
                    the taking of it back. . . .

The Homeric Hymns, Greek (c. 6500 B.C.)

Chandrakot, Nepal

S A T U R D A Y

Vespers

Pilgrimage to the place of the wise is to escape the
flame of separation from Nature.

Old Sufi saying

For in their hearts doth Nature stir them so,
Then people long on pilgrimage to go,
And palmers to be seeking foreign strands,
To distant shrines renowned in sundry lands.

Geoffrey Chaucer,
English (c. 1342–1400)

Yangshuo, China

SATURDAY

Compline

When each day
is sacred

when each hour
is sacred

when each instant
is sacred

earth and you
space and you
bearing the sacred
through time

you'll reach
the fields of light.

Guillevic,
Breton (1907–   )

Glastonbury Tor, Somersetshire, England

THE HIDDEN IMAGE

The sound stops short, the sense flows on.

Old Chinese saying

My work came out of years of travel throughout the world, during which I developed a fascination with the monumental, the earth's ancient and powerful symbols and the messages that they left for us. At some unknown point, I heard a restless voice tell me that behind that pillar is something else. In my search for this hidden image, I began to sense that within the apparent visual harmony there was a life force that inhabited the physical form, a deeper pulse that I could hear only when I allowed myself to be in a state of quiet watchfulness. I saw form as a place-mark for this familiar presence that manifested itself in the sites and faces I encountered on my journeys. I came to recognize this presence, this cumulative experience, this soul of the world. Through a process of subtraction I have attempted to strip away the physical elements in order to reveal their essential core of emotion and significance. I have sought out images that compel a transition from the feeling of the immediate to the experience of timelessness.

Eric Lawton
Los Angeles

PHOTOGRAPHS

S U N D A Y

Matins: Sunrise, Chandrakot, Nepal (1985). On the trail to Annapurna, the path through this luminous, mountain-ringed glacier basin in the Himalaya passes through forest and labyrinthine valleys.

Lauds: Sunrise, Pokhara, Nepal (1985). The Himalayan trade route for the hill people, including Tibetans, Sherpas, and Gurungs, this steep path is worn into the mountain. There are no roads west of Pokhara, which has been called the last outpost of the modern world.

Prime: Light Through Snow Trees, Taos, New Mexico (1987). Near the village of Chimayo, known for centuries by the Indians and Spanish colonists as a healing ground.

Terce: Two Women, Machapuchare, Nepal (1976). The sacred peak of Machapuchare (22,958 feet) has never been climbed. Nepali legend holds that twin goddesses reside on the mountain peak.

Sext: Taj Mahal, Agra, India (1976). Built by the Mogul emperor Shah Jahan in 1632–1649 to immortalize his queen, Mumtaz Mahal, the Taj Mahal is also a place of pilgrimage. Standing above the Yamuna River, it is a symbol of order and harmony.

None: Temple Pond, Suzhou, China (1988). An ancient Chinese proverb states, "In Heaven there is Paradise, on Earth there is Suzhou." Suzhou's ancient gardens date back 2,500 years. The garden's symbolic nature is suggestive of the ebb and flow of the waters of life.

Vespers: Man at Peak, Yuping-Lou, Huangshan, China (1988). Yuping-Lou was originally the Temple of the Bodhisattva of Wisdom. This peak is reached after climbing thousands of stone steps. Pilgrims have sought inspiration from the granite, mist, and pines for more than a thousand years.

Compline: Fog Forest, Huangshan, China (1988). For centuries, Chinese poets and painters have immortalized the four ultimate beauties of Huangshan: ancient pines clinging to the rock face, fantastically shaped rocks, the "Sea of Clouds and Fog," and the hot springs.

MONDAY

Matins: Man in Forest, Yangshuo, China (1988). A forest on a hill whose peaks form a pattern similar to that of the stars in the Big Dipper. Also known as "The Forest of Tablets," nearby caves contain carved inscriptions dating back to the Tang and Ming dynasties.

Lauds: Sunrise, Kanchenjunga, from Darjeeling, India (1985). The world's third highest peak at 28,208 feet, Kanchenjunga divides Darjeeling, Sikkim, Nepal, and Bhutan in the eastern Himalaya. Tradition says that it is the abode of the "Five Sacred Treasures of the Great Snow" buried by the god Kanchenjunga: salt, gems, sacred books, medicines, and an impenetrable suit of armor.

Prime: Sinai Desert (1978). The sacred land where Moses led the Israelites through four decades of lost trails and new paths to the promised land.

Terce: Old Man with Child, Yangshuo, China (1988). Near the Zengpigan cave, the site of a Stone Age village some ten thousand years ago.

Sext: Kalalau Valley, Kauai, Hawaii (1981). Along the ancient Na Pali Trail, this valley contains stonework ruins from the old civilization where sacred rites were practiced and landlocked villagers traded in harmony with fishing villages that had no fresh water.

None: Two Pilgrims, Huangshan, China (1988). Huangshan has been a site of pilgrimage for thousands of years. Writers and artists describe it as "walking into an unending Chinese landscape painting." The Chinese believe that ascending such peaks heightens the spirit.

Vespers: Eagle, Masai Mara, Kenya (1977). The wild savannas of Masai Mara open onto the Serengeti Plain of Tanzania at the foot of Mount Kilimanjaro.

Compline: Moon and Crosses, Taos Pueblo, New Mexico (1981). Taos Pueblo is an ancient and historic site, framed by the sacred Taos Mountains. Centuries before the Spanish conquest, the Indians regarded this land as the spiritual dwelling of their ancestors.

Matins: Trees, Mountain Peaks, Chandrakot, Nepal (1985). On the Himalayan Trail to Annapurna, misted pine forests give way to deep gorges split by roaring rivers.

Lauds: Temple Sunrise, Guilin, China (1988). Guilin's landscape of karst formations, thrust up from the limestone seabed over 300 million years ago, is unique in China and the rest of the world and is immortalized in Chinese painting and poetry.

Prime: Gate House, Cayucos, California (1981). Between Morro Bay and San Simeon, this area was inhabited by Indians for thousands of years.

Terce: Temple Tower, Wuxi, China (1988). Wuxi's long history dates back some three thousand years to the Shang and Zhou periods, when scattered settlements existed.

Sext: Inca Trail to Machu Picchu, Peru (1987). The ancient Inca trail winds through junglelike cloud forests and 14,000-foot mountain passes filled with Incan ruins. It culminates at the Inti Puntu, or Gate of the Sun, through which one enters Machu Picchu, the "City of Light."

None: Light and Clouds, Death Valley, California (1988). The name Death Valley is forbidding, yet the magical quality of the elements here is awe-inspiring.

Vespers: Chairs in Cathedral, Copenhagen, Denmark (1986).

Compline: Moon over Stonehenge, England (1990). Stonehenge is believed to have been built four thousand years ago in an open landscape strewn with burial mounds, earthworks, and many other prehistoric monuments. The entire area is imprinted with the marks of ancient sanctity. Above all, builders of Stonehenge were concerned with keeping the lives of the people in time with the seasons and rhythms of nature.

Matins: Man and Mountain, Pfeiffer Beach, Big Sur, California (1984). The Esselen Indians and their forebears have held this land sacred for centuries.

Lauds: Tracks Through Field, Salisbury Plain, England (1990). Near the high, earth-walled eminence called Old Sarum. Its outer ramparts are prehistoric, and its occupants have included Iron Age Britons, Romans, Saxons, and Normans. It once was an important religious center.

Prime: Stairway, Jutland Lighthouse, Denmark (1986). Shaped by the wind and the sand, a sand dune was formed so high that the light could no longer be seen from the sea. The surrounding landscape contains 5,000-year-old Stone Age graves and Viking fortifications and settlements.

Terce: House on Water, Chincoteague, Virginia (1980). Chincoteague Island is a small forest filled with wild ponies. This small house stands on stilts off its shore.

Sext: Pond, Hanalei, Kauai, Hawaii (1981). Hawaiian legends describe the kahuna (the "Guardians of the Mysteries"), ancient keepers of wisdom whose presence may still be felt.

None: Sunrise Clouds over Stonehenge, England (1990). The solar and lunar orientation of Stonehenge identifies it as a temple to the sun and moon, worshiped as symbols of the two great principles in nature, the male and female archetypes. The heat and splendor of the sun represent positively charged energy; the moon represents the negative pole. The sun and moon are related to heaven and earth; the first as active and fertile, the second as receptive and fruitful.

Vespers: Man and Glacier, Pastoruri, Huascarán, Peru (1987). At 16,000 feet Pastoruri Glacier is near Mount Huascarán (22,198 feet) in Peru's highest Andean range, the Cordillera Blanca.

Compline: Blue Layers, Dhampus, Nepal (1985). A land of deep purple shadows, ravines, and emptiness. Legends speak of Shambhala, the center of the world, which exists in this Himalaya. Tradition says that the venerable Lao-tzu, having given the Tao to the Keeper of the Pass, vanished with his ox into such emptiness.

Matins: Moon and Three Mountains, Santa Fe, New Mexico (1987). Near the cave dwellings and stone houses of the Anasazi, ancestors of the Pueblo Indians. An important part of Anasazi culture was an underground structure called a kiva. They believed that through it their ancestors entered this world from a world below.

Lauds: Storm and Sea, Bahamas (1988). For centuries ships coming from South America carrying Incan wealth to Spain were thrown by typhoons and a dark and angry sea onto the shallow Bahamian shoals.

Prime: Sunrise, Yangshuo, China (1988). According to legend, this region was once inhabited by fierce beasts and demons. A huge man appeared one day and slew a giant demon with a single arrow, freeing the region of demons forever.

Terce: Zabriskie Point, Death Valley, California (1988). The rock layers comprise a nearly complete record of the earth's past. These ancient rock layers have only risen in recent geological times.

Sext: Stone Steps, Machu Picchu, Peru (1987). In ancient times, the Incan "City of Light" could be entered only by persons who, through study and meditation, had reconciled themselves with death and understood the lessons of immortality.

None: Monks, Punakha Monastery, Bhutan (1985). In remote Wangdi Valley, Punakha Dzong is a centuries-old fortress-monastery; it was the ancient capital of Bhutan and houses many sacred temples. Lying between India and Tibet, secluded by some of the world's highest mountains for thousands of years of solitude, this medieval kingdom is known as "The Land of the Thunder Dragon."

Vespers: Boats, Hiroshima, Japan (1976). From the spot of ground zero in the atomic blast, new life rises from the river like the phoenix, to begin anew.

Compline: Sky and Sea, Hanalei, Kauai, Hawaii (1981). On the horizon is the Hoku-le'a, a replica of the oceangoing canoes by which ancient seafaring Polynesians voyaged over two thousand miles across the South Seas to Hawaii sometime between A.D. 500 and 800. They navigated without instruments, fixing on two key stars: Sirius and Arcturus, which they called Hoku-le'a.

Matins: Foot, Suzhou, China (1988). For thousands of years, travelers have passed through this city of canals, described by Marco Polo as "The Venice of the East."

Lauds: Desert Presence, Death Valley, California (1988). Death Valley was formed millions of years ago when the folds of the earth's crust uplifted surrounding mountains and depressed the valley to eight hundred feet below sea level. Evaporating Ice Age lakes left this barren landscape.

Prime: Temple of Poseidon, Cape Sounion, Greece (1972). This fifth-century B.C. cliff-top temple overlooks the Aegean Sea and inspired Lord Byron in his travels.

Terce: Lake Titicaca at Puno, Peru (1987). Dividing Peru and Bolivia, at 13,000 feet it is the highest navigable lake in the world. The Incans believed that God took mankind out of the lake and placed him in this abstract world of the *altiplano.* Fed by the melting snows of the Andes, the lake contains the Incan Islands of the Sun and the Moon.

Sext: Blue Louvre, Paris, France (1983). Originally a twelfth-century fort, the Louvre was the palace of French kings from the fourteenth century and is now the national art gallery of France. Its development parallels the growth of Paris.

None: Yangtze River, China (1988). The longest river in China at over three thousand miles, the Yangtze rises in the mountains of southwest China and flows to the East China Sea. Legend says that twelve stone goddesses guide ships along the river, and when a goddess emerges from the mist, she brings good luck to anyone who glimpses her.

Vespers: Family Group, Paro Valley, Bhutan (1985). Fed by the snows of Mount Chomo Lhari, the glacier waters from its five Himalayan sister peaks stream in torrents through deep gorges, converging into the Paro Chu River to nourish Paro Valley to life. There the Taktsang Monastery, or Tiger's Nest, is built around a cave where Guru Padma Sambhava is said to have brought Buddhism to Bhutan by flying in on the back of a tiger.

Compline: Tunnel, Guanajuato, Mexico (1980). Founded in 1548, Guanajuato's silver mines are fabled. The city is hunched on the slopes of a rugged, narrow canyon. The entry is through a subterranean stone tunnel that follows the original course of the Guanajuato River under the city.

Matins: Crosses, Ninth-Century Church, Dordogne Valley, France (1983). This church in southwestern France is surrounded by caves deep in the bowels of the earth in which Cro-Magnon cave paintings date back to 30,000 B.C.

Lauds: Pillars, Santa Monica, California (1985).

Prime: Moon and Dune, Death Valley, California (1988). In the harshness and severity of this environment, this primordial landscape supports more than nine hundred kinds of life.

Terce: Blue Fog Trees, Graves, Virginia (1980).

Sext: Rhumtek Monastery, Gangtok, Sikkim (1985). One of the great monasteries of Tibetan Buddhism, this Himalayan mountaintop has been for centuries the abode of the holy Karmapa.

None: Woman with a Basket, Chandrakot, Nepal (1985). This woman has risen before dawn to tend her fields as her forebears have done for countless generations before her.

Vespers: Bicycles, Yangshuo, China (1988). Throughout this primordial karst landscape are mud-walled villages where the ethnic Zhang minorities have farmed the land for centuries.

Compline: Glastonbury Tor, Somersetshire, England (1990). Pilgrims are drawn to this place of magic, legend, and natural enchantment, which may be the mythical Avalon of the Arthurian legends. The top of the tor has been the site of pagan temples, Saxon churches, and finally Saint Michael's Church, of which a tower survives. The ridges that circle the hill may be the remains of an early Christian ritual path that winds around the hill seven times.

CREDITS

Grateful acknowledgment is made as follows for permission to reprint copyrighted material:

To Dr. Ira Progoff, copyright © 1983, for his translation of *The Cloud of Unknowing,* Laurel Books, published by Dell Publishing Co., a Division of Bantam, Doubleday, Dell Inc. Reprinted with permission of the publisher.

To Stephen Mitchell, copyright © 1989, for his translation of Lao-tzu from the *Tao Te Ching,* and for Psalm 19, Han-shan, and The Revelation of St. John from *The Enlightened Heart,* HarperCollins Publishers. Reprinted by permission from HarperCollins Publishers.

Excerpt from *Holy the Firm,* by Annie Dillard. Copyright © 1977. Reprinted by permission from HarperCollins Publishers.

To Threshold Books for excerpts from *Open Secret: Versions of Rumi,* translated by John Moyne and Coleman Barks, copyright © by Threshold Books, 1984.

To Robert Bly, for his translations of Kabīr from *The Kabīr Book,* The Seventies Press, copyright © 1977; for translations of Rainer Maria Rilke, from *Selected Poems of Rainer Maria Rilke,* HarperCollins, copyright © 1981.

Permission to quote from *Meditations with Hildegard of Bingen,* versions and introduction by Gabriele Uhlein, copyright © 1983 by Bear & Company, Inc.

For excerpt from *Markings,* by Dag Hammarskjöld. Copyright © 1964 by Alfred A. Knopf, Inc., and Faber and Faber, Ltd. Foreword copyright by W. H. Auden. Translated from the Swedish by Leif Sjoberg and W. H. Auden. Ballantine Books. Reprinted by permission of the Dag Hammarskjöld estate.

Permission to quote from *Black Elk Speaks,* as told through John G. Neihardt, copyright © 1959 by Washington Square Books.

Permission to quote from *Souls on Fire,* by Elie Wiesel, copyright © 1972 by Elie Wiesel. Translated from the French by Marion Wiesel. Reprinted by permission from Summit Books.

Isak Dinesen, from *Out of Africa.* Copyright © 1937 by Random House, Inc., and renewed 1965 by Rungstedlundfonden. Reprinted by permission of Random House, Inc., and the Rungstedlund Foundation.